the New

EXPERIENCING BREAKTHROUGH
ON EVERY LEVEL

Mark & Trina Hankins

Unless otherwise indicated, all scriptural quotations are from the King James Version of the Bible.

ISBN 978-1-889981-59-8

Published by MHM Publications
P.O. Box 12863
Alexandria, LA 71315

TABLE OF CONTENTS

REVELATION
FROM GOD
WILL FUEL DEDICATION
TO GOD!

1

Break Every Barrier

Chuck Yeager was the young, daredevil pilot who volunteered to fly the jet that would attempt to break the sound barrier. After many test flights and adjustments, he flew supersonic. When the first sonic boom was heard, everyone thought his jet had crashed. Instead, he circled back triumphant and later went on to break more flight records. He said this about flying supersonic: ***"The real barrier was not in the sky. It was in our knowledge of supersonic flight."***

How true this is for us as believers also. The real barrier is in our knowledge—or lack thereof. But it is a new day in the Church! It is a day of revelation knowledge that will cause breakthrough on every level! It has already begun. Isaiah 43:18–19 (AMP) says, *"Do not [earnestly] remember the former things; neither consider the things of old. Behold, I am doing a* **new thing!** *Now it springs forth; do you not perceive and know it and will you not give heed to it? I will even make a way in the wilderness and rivers in the desert."* The New Living Translation says, *"For I am about to do* **something new.** *See, I have already begun! Do you not see it?"* Hallelujah! God is doing a new thing!

MORE REVELATION

When I was a young man, I wanted to follow God. I wanted to live right. But I often found myself going in the wrong direction. I rededicated my life to God so many times my "dedicator" wore out! Then I heard Brother Kenneth E. Hagin teach on how to pray Ephesians 1:16–23:

> *I cease not to give thanks for you, making mention of you in my prayers; That the God of our Lord Jesus Christ, the Father of glory, may give unto you the spirit of wisdom and revelation in the knowledge of him: <u>The eyes of your understanding being enlightened; that ye may know</u> what is the*

hope of his calling, and what the riches of the glory of his inheritance in the saints, And what is the exceeding greatness of his power to us-ward who believe, according to the working of his mighty power, Which he wrought in Christ, when he raised him from the dead, and set him at his own right hand in the heavenly places, Far above all principality, and power, and might, and dominion, and every name that is named, not only in this world, but also in that which is to come: And hath put all things under his feet, and gave him to be the head over all things to the church, Which is his body, the fulness of him that filleth all in all.

Praying this prayer for 6 months would make the Bible a different book to those who did. Brother Hagin said I should pray these scriptures every day for six months if I wanted my life to be different. I began that day and found out he was right. **I did not need more dedication. I needed more revelation**, just as this prayer says. You see, I found out that revelation **FROM** God will fuel dedication **TO** God. Instead of praying for more dedication, I began to pray for more *revelation*. This changed everything for me!

It is said there are three times a person changes in life:

> 1. *When they hurt badly enough that they have to.*
> 2. *When the rewards are great enough that they want to.*
> 3. *When they learn enough that they are able to.*

As believers, the Holy Spirit reveals to us the knowledge we need to be free and to make real changes through Christ.

Romans 8:2 (Phillips) says, *"For the new spiritual principle of life in Christ Jesus lifts me out of the old vicious circle of sin and death."* Just as the law of lift overcomes the law of gravity to enable airplanes to fly, the higher spiritual law called the "law of the Spirit of life in Christ Jesus" overcomes sin and enables believers to reign in life. As I prayed the Ephesians 1 prayer and gained revelation knowledge, I found God that was working in me,

PTL

14

giving me the desire and power to do His will (Phil. 2:13).

THIS CHANGES EVERYTHING

Albert Einstein's theory of relativity, $E=mc^2$, was a breakthrough in knowledge. It made old information obsolete and changed everything previously taught. Einstein apologized to Sir Isaac Newton because this new theory made Mr. Newton's theories irrelevant.

Just as Einstein's theory changed everything, Jesus, the Firstborn of a new kind of humanity, broke every barrier on a much greater, eternal scale. This changes everything for you and me! Because of Jesus, we can live differently than the rest of the world. We can live victorious and free. Jesus made all things new! But we have a part to play too.

A CALL FOR PIONEERS

The old, American pioneer trails were littered with furniture and other household items that were simply too heavy to carry across the mountains. As they traveled, the pioneers realized there were things they needed to take and things they needed to leave behind.

As believers, there are some things we need to leave behind in order to move forward with God. Acknowledging your identification with Christ will separate you from your past— from the things you shouldn't carry. Strip off those weights and sins. Leave them behind so you can run your race and finish your course with joy (Heb. 12:1).

I like to say that there are **three kinds of people: pioneers, settlers, and**

museum keepers. Museum keepers are content to brush off the memories of the past. Settlers have gone as far as they want to go. They just want to settle in their comfort zone. Then there are the pioneers who say, "I know there is more to discover. I am not content to stop here or live in the past."

I believe Heaven is calling us to press forward, increase our borders, and change our world. Let's be pioneers for Christ.

GOD HAS AN EVER-INCREASING PLAN FOR YOUR LIFE

Our daughter, Alicia, was talking to her son Landon before he went to sleep one night. She told him, "You know, Landon, God has a plan for your life." Immediately, Landon jumped up and shouted, "He does? Well, what is it?"

We should all be this excited! I am telling you now, God has a plan for your life! Do not just yawn and say, "I have heard that before. No! Get ready for the biggest changes you have ever experienced in your life!

FORGET ABOUT
WHAT'S HAPPENED;
DON'T KEEP GOING
OVER OLD HISTORY.
BE ALERT, BE PRESENT.
***I'M ABOUT TO DO
SOMETHING BRAND-NEW.***
IT'S BURSTING OUT!
DON'T YOU SEE IT?
THERE IT IS! I'M MAKING
A ROAD THROUGH
THE DESERT, RIVERS
IN THE BADLANDS.

ISAIAH 43:18-19 (MESSAGE)

2

Prepare for
the New

As Joshua led Israel into the Promised Land, he told the people to get ready to go where they had never gone before. He gave them three days to prepare themselves to leave the wilderness, cross over the Jordan, possess new territory, kill giants, and take cities. Joshua

3:4–5 says, *"Ye have not passed this way heretofore. And Joshua said unto the people, Sanctify yourselves: for to morrow the Lord will do wonders among you."* After wandering in the wilderness for 40 years, it was time to prepare. It was time to fulfill God's plan.

Preparation time is so important. Abraham Lincoln said, "I will study; I will prepare, and my opportunity will come." Now is the time to prepare! Now is the time to sanctify yourself for God to do wonders that will eclipse any trouble you experienced in the last year. **God is doing a new thing**

in you. Your opportunity is now!

What exactly does it mean to sanctify yourself? The word *sanctify* means "to make holy, to purify, to cleanse, to set apart, and to consecrate." It means to set apart something or someone for a special purpose. Sanctification means not only separation from sin but also separation from what may be permissible. It is an act of God.

P.C. Nelson, a Bible scholar, said this about sanctification:

Sanctification is realized in the believer by recognizing

his identification with Christ in His death, burial and resurrection, and by faith reckoning daily upon the fact of union with Christ, and by offering daily every faculty continually to the dominion of the Holy Spirit.

In other words, sanctification begins with the work God did for us in the death, burial, and resurrection of Christ. Jesus identified with us. Identification means to treat or consider as one and the same. I like to think of identification with Christ as a group picture. Who is the first person you look for in a group picture? Yourself. In the same way, when you look into the scriptures you want to see yourself identified completely within Jesus. Being identified with Christ means you were there with Him on His cross. Jesus' victory is also your victory!

There is an old hymn that asks, "Were you there when they crucified my Lord?" When I heard that song as a boy, I thought, "No, I wasn't there. I didn't do it. That was 2,000 years ago. I was not even in

Jerusalem." While it is true that none of us were there physically, we were there in Christ. This is an eternal God event which can be visited at any point in time. It is not just a historical or geographical event—it is a spiritual reality. And as that hymn says, it does cause us to tremble!

Did you ever think about the difference between a photo and an x-ray? They provide completely different images, even of the same object or person. You sure would not want to send out an x-ray of your family for

Christmas! Identification with Christ can be compared to the difference between a photo and an x-ray. In Christ, you just see things differently.

Likewise, the four gospels are a photograph of our redemption in Christ and the epistles are an x-ray. In the gospels, we see that Jesus was crucified, buried, and raised from the dead. We see what God saw in the spirit in the epistles, **we died with Christ.** Galatian 2:20 says, "Christ took me to the cross with Him and I died there with Him" (Laubach). Another translation says, "I consider myself as having died and now enjoying a second existence, which is simply Jesus using my body" (Distilled).

Romans 6:4 says that *we were buried with Christ*. Romans 6:11 says *to reckon ourselves dead* to sin. One translation says, "you are dead to sin...motionless as a corpse." What a picture! But we did not stay dead. Romans 6:4 continues, "We have been *justified and raised with Him* by the glory of God." And according to Romans 6:14, sin shall not have dominion over us in Christ. We were dead, but Christ made us alive in Him. Galatians 2:20 says, "It is no longer I who lives, but Christ Who lives in me." Not only that, but now *we are seated with Him and reign as kings* in life (Eph. 2:6, Rom. 5:17).

Romans 6:4 in its entirety says: *"Therefore we are buried with him by baptism into death: that like as Christ was raised up from the dead by the glory of the Father, even so we also should walk in newness of life."* This is the way God enables us to walk in a new life.

STOP LOOKING IN
THE YEARBOOK
OF THE PAST

If you want to experience your new identity in Christ, you cannot keep looking in the yearbook of the past. You are dead to all that. But **the devil knows that if he can challenge your identity, he will hinder your destiny.** Now is the time to sanctify yourself and establish your identity in Christ. Do not wait! Condemnation, fear, and bondage are gone! Johnson's translation of Romans 8:1 says,

"Now there is no accusing voice nagging those who are united to Christ." It is a new day! Now is the time to rise and shine. Your light is come, and the glory of the Lord is risen upon you (Isaiah 61:1)!

THE THINGS
WE REFUSE TO
SEPARATE
FROM ARE THE
THINGS THAT WILL
SEPARATE
US FROM THE
WILL OF GOD!

3

The Cross Forms a Permanent Barrier Against Sin

When Trina and I went on a tour of Israel, one very interesting site we visited was the security wall. It was built in Jerusalem to protect citizens from terrorists who were coming into their neighborhoods and killing innocent people. This wall is 26 feet high and 330 feet wide in some places.

Like that wall, the cross has formed a barrier to protect anyone who is "in Christ" from the world and sin. Galatians 6:14 says, *"But far be it from me to boast about anything except the cross of our head Jesus Christ: that cross forms a permanent barrier (to erect a fence) between the world and me, and between me and the world" (Bruce).*

Acknowledging your identification with Christ is the way to separate yourself from sin and its power in your life. The cross brings sin to an end. The old creation is destroyed and there is a resurrection provided whereby there is a complete continuation of Christ's victory.

The antibodies in the body that have overcome a disease contain memory cells. Those cells carry the memory of how it defeated that disease. One drop of blood contains the history of any disease an individual has overcome. One drop of Jesus' blood contains the total history of all He has overcome for us. **Jesus' blood contains the memory cell of how it defeated sin and any fault.** When sin tries to enter your life, you apply or plead the blood and it has no power!

SANCTIFIED BY
THE BLOOD AND
THE HOLY SPIRIT

The Holy Spirit and the blood always go together. In 1 Peter 1:2, it says it is *"through sanctification of the Spirit, unto obedience and sprinkling of the blood of Jesus Christ."* The blood of Jesus cleanses your conscience by the power of the Holy Spirit. There is wonder-working power in the blood!

"Neither by the blood of goats and calves, but by his own blood he entered in once into the holy place, having

obtained eternal redemption for us. For if the blood of bulls and of goats, and the ashes of an heifer sprinkling the unclean, sanctifieth to the purifying of the flesh: <u>How much more shall the blood of Christ, who through the eternal Spirit</u> offered himself without spot to God, purge your conscience from dead works to serve the living God?"

-Hebrews 9:12–14

NOT MY WILL

When Jesus prayed in the garden, *"Not my will, but Thine,*

be done" (Luke 22:42), He was sanctifying His own will and humbling Himself to the plan of redemption. His obedience broke the curse that came from Adam's disobedience. Now, like Him, we sanctify our will and present our bodies for Him to use—a living sacrifice, holy and acceptable to God (Rom. 12:1).

We must humble ourselves in order to go higher. Even the Apostle Paul practiced this lifestyle. He said in 1 Corinthians 9:27, "But I keep under my body, and bring it into subjection: lest that by any means, when I have preached to others, I myself should be a castaway." When we submit ourselves to Him to purge, or cleanse us, we can move in to new territory in our prayer lives, personal lives, relationships, work, and ministry.

HOW TO BECOME A VESSEL OF HONOR

This process of purging and cleansing is not only on God's side. We must take responsibility to separate ourselves from iniquity and become vessels of honor. Look at what Paul told Timothy:

Nevertheless the foundation of God standeth sure, having this seal, The Lord knoweth them that are his. And, let every one that nameth the name of Christ depart from iniquity. But in a great house there are not only vessels of gold and of silver, but also of wood and of earth; and some to honour, and some to dishonour. If a man therefore purge himself from these, he shall be a vessel unto honour, sanctified, and meet for the master's use, and prepared unto every good work.

-2 Timothy 2:19–21

Jesus, the Head of the Church, wants us to be vessels of honor God can use. The Holy Spirit brings us to a point of obedience. But we must take responsibility to cleanse ourselves. *"Having therefore these promises, dearly beloved, let us cleanse ourselves from all filthiness of the flesh and spirit, perfecting holiness in the fear of God" (2 Cor. 7:1).* **The things we refuse to separate from are the things that will separate us from the will of God.**

All Jesus did for us in redemption is in His blood. Naturally speaking, our DNA (our identification) is in our blood. But when the blood of Jesus cleanses us, it literally purges and washes our "genes." Hebrews 10:22 says, *"Let us draw near with a true heart in full assurance of faith, having our hearts sprinkled from an evil conscience, and our bodies washed with pure water."* Jesus makes us brand new!

NOT VICTIMS, BUT VICTORS

In the letters to the Church, the Epistles, no one is called a victim. Instead, Paul tells us we have the power to purge ourselves. That means you and

I are not helpless victims. The word *victim* comes from the root word *wicca*, which is Latin for the word *witch*. It represents a person or animal used in sacrificial worship (Webster's Dictionary). In Christ, we are no longer victims. Jesus became sin and through His blood broke the curse and purchased our complete freedom from Satan's power. In Him, we are victors! A victor is one who defeats the enemy or opponent.

Start declaring that today. "I am victorious in Christ!" You overcome by the blood of the Lamb and the Word of your testimony (Rev. 12:11). Your testimony releases sanctifying power. As 2 Corinthians 5:17 (AMP) says, *"The old previous moral and spiritual condition has passed away. Behold the fresh and new has begun."* Jesus Christ makes you **new**!

THEREFORE,
IF ANY MAN
BE **IN CHRIST,**
HE IS A **NEW
CREATURE**:
OLD THINGS ARE
PASSED AWAY;
BEHOLD, ALL
THINGS ARE
BECOME NEW.

2 CORINTHIANS 5:17 (KJV)

4

Promulgate: Making It Legal

There are two ordinances in the Church which demonstrate our identification with Christ: water baptism and communion. We know that water baptism represents being buried with Christ and risen with Him to walk in newness of life. And the Apostle Paul refers to communion as the "cup of blessing" (1 Cor. 10:16). In fact, communion or what we call, the Lord's Supper, shows or proclaims our union with Christ in His body and His blood.

In 1 Corinthians 11:26 it says, *"For as often as ye eat this bread, and drink this cup, ye do shew the Lord's death till he come."* Look at the word *shew*. It is *kataggello* in the Greek and means "to proclaim, **promulgate**, declare, and preach." Promulgate means to "put (a law or decree) into effect by official proclamation."

This same word is used in Colossians 2:15. *"And having spoiled principalities and powers, he [Jesus] made a shew of them openly, triumphing over them in it."* Jesus was publicly proclaiming His complete defeat of Satan's kingdom and our complete victory in His resurrection. And if we are going to live like Him, it is time we start declaring some things too. *It is time to promulgate!*

Declare these things right now: "I have been crucified with Christ. It is no longer I who live, but Christ Who lives in me. I live by the faith of the Son of God. I am dead to sin. The old person has died, and sin has no dominion over me. I am enjoying a new existence, which is Jesus using my body. I am a new creation. The old is gone and I'm living a fresh, new life!"

A NEW SEASON

This is your season to be healed and made new! In 2 Corinthians 5:17 it says if any man be in Christ he is a new creation. The New Living Bible says he is *"a brand new person inside."* Another translation says, *"a new world has at once opened upon him, an old world has passed away (Stanter)."* The New Engish Bible says, *"the old order has gone, and a new order has already begun."*

The Amplified Bible translates

this, *"if any man is engrafted in Christ."* In horticulture, grafting takes place to strengthen a plant, change varieties, or to cause two different plants to grow together as one. However, there can be no grafting without first wounding them.

Likewise, Jesus was wounded so we could be engrafted into Him. Isaiah 53:5–6 tells us, *"Surely he hath borne our griefs, and carried our sorrows: yet we did esteem him stricken, smitten of God, and afflicted. But he was wounded for our transgressions, he was bruised for our iniquities: the chastisement of our peace was upon him; and with his stripes we are healed."*

The word *borne* is the Hebrew word *nasa*, which means "to lift." Jesus has lifted our sorrows and has taken our torment so that we can have perfect peace.

We do not have to be bound by shame, rejection, or feelings of abandonment. Instead, we can let the cleansing blood of Jesus heal us where we have been wounded by life. That blood will silence the accuser's voice that tells us, "It's your fault." It will stop all self-condemnation. Some of the most powerful words are those found in Hebrews 2:14–15: *"...through death he might destroy him that had the power of death, that is, the devil; And deliver them who through fear of death were all their lifetime subject to bondage."* We have been delivered by the precious blood of Jesus!

It is time to promulgate! Declare right now: "I am a completely new person in Christ. The old person I was is gone. There is a new world opened to me where all things are new. By Jesus' wounds I am healed and engrafted into Him. He has lifted my sorrows and griefs. I am no longer bound by fear! I now have perfect peace."

BE **CONSTANTLY RENEWED** IN THE SPIRIT OF YOUR MIND [HAVING A FRESH MENTAL AND SPIRITUAL ATTITUDE].

EPHESIANS 4:24 (AMP)

5

Get Out of the Ruts You've Been Stuck In

There was a warning sign on a remote and muddy road marked by deep ruts that said, "Be careful of the ruts you get in because you could be stuck in them for the next 60 miles." That is a long time to be stuck! It has been proven that we have similar ruts in our brains from repeated ways of thinking. But there is a way to get out of those ruts we have been stuck in. And that is through sanctification.

Sanctification happens when we daily "reckon" on the reality of our union with Christ. The word *reckon* is an accounting term meaning to record the facts. It is daily and continually offering every faculty—including our minds—continually to the dominion of the Holy Spirit. We are transformed by the renewing of our minds (Eph. 4:23).

The Jerusalem Bible says in Ephesians 4:23 our mind must undergo a spiritual revolution.

The first thing that takes place in a revolution is a complete takeover of communication. Philemon 6 says when we acknowledge every good thing which is in us in Christ, our faith will become effective and contagious. People around us will see a difference. They will catch our faith.

YOU CAN HAVE A FRESH MENTAL ATTITUDE

God wants to do a work in your mind and imagination. Ephesians 4:24 (AMP) says, *"Be constantly renewed in the spirit of your mind [having a fresh mental and spiritual attitude]."* Hebrews 10:16 follows this thought: *"This is the covenant that I will make with them after those days, said the Lord, I will put my laws into their hearts, and in their minds will I write them."* The Amplified Bible says, *"on their mind will I inscribe them (producing an inward change)."*

This new life in Christ comes with a new way of thinking which brings a totally new lifestyle. What you struggled with in your past will be no more.

The Lord is good, a strong hold in the day of trouble; and he knoweth them that trust in him. But with an overrunning flood he will make an utter end of the place thereof, and darkness shall pursue his enemies... he will make an utter end: affliction shall not rise up the second time.

-Nahum 1:8–9

Sin and affliction have come to an end! That enemy will never come back.

So if anyone becomes united to Christ, he is a fresh Creation; the original conditions have passed away; mark! they have been replaced by new conditions.

-2 Cor. 5:17 (Wade)

...he becomes a new person altogether—the past is finished and gone, everything has become fresh and new.

-Phillips

Forget about what's happened; don't keep going

*over old history. Be alert,
be present. I'm about to do
something brand-new. It's
bursting out! Don't you see
it? There it is! I'm making
a road through the desert,
rivers in the badlands.*
-Isa. 43:18-19 (Message)

The power of the cross brings old things to an end. God has a new plan for your life! It is a dawning of a new day! The accuser must be silent. The enemies of fear, anxiety, shame, and guilt will never rise and come back to haunt you. You've put your trust in the blood of

Jesus, you're sanctifying yourself, and God is making a way where there was no way. Get ready for the new!

REFERENCES

The Amplified Bible. Zondervan Publishing House, Grand Rapids, Michigan, 1972.

Bruce, F.F. *The Letters of Paul, An Expanded Paraphrase.* Eerdmans Publishing Company, Grand Rapids, Michigan, 1965. ✳

The Distilled Bible/New Testament. Paul Benjamin Publishing Company, Stone Mountain, Georgia, 1980.

The Jerusalem Bible. Double Day and Company, Inc., New York, New York, 1968.

Johnson, Ben Campbell. *The Heart of Paul, A Rational Paraphrase of the New Testament.* Word Books, Waco, Texas, 1976.

Laubach, Frank C. *The Inspired Letters in Clearest English.* Thomas Nelson and Sons, New York, New York, 1956.

New Living Translation. Tyndale House Publishers. Wheaton, Ill: 1996.

Nelson, P.C. *Bible Doctrines.* Gospel Publishing House, Springfield, Missouri, 1971.

New English Bible. Oxford University Press, Oxford, England, 1961.

Peterson, Eugene. *The Message/Remix, The Bible in Contemporary Language.* NavPress Publishing Group, Colorado Springs, Colorado, 2003.

Phillips, J.B. *The New Testament in Modern English.* The Macmillan Company, New York, New York, 1958.

Strong, James. *The New Strong Exhaustive* ✳
Concordance of the Bible, 2003.

Wade, G.W. *The Documents of the* ✳
New Testament. Thomas Burby and
Company, London, England, 1934.

Webster-dictionary.net. (2018). *Webster
Dictionary.* [online] Available at: http://
www.webster-dictionary.net/

ACKNOWLEDGMENTS

Special thanks to my wife, Trina.

My son, Aaron and his wife, Errin Cody; their daughters, Avery Jane and Macy Claire, their son, Jude Aaron.

My daughter, Alicia and her husband, Caleb; their sons, Jaiden Mark, Gavin Luke, Landon James, and Dylan Paul, their daughter Hadley Marie.

My parents, Pastor B.B. and Velma Hankins, who are now in Heaven with the Lord.

My wife's parents, Rev. William and Ginger Behrman.

ABOUT THE AUTHORS

Mark and Trina Hankins travel nationally & internationally preaching the Word of God with the power of the Holy Spirit. Their message centers on the spirit of faith, who the believer is in Christ, and the work of the Holy Spirit.

After over forty years of pastoral and traveling ministry, Mark and Trina are now ministering full-time in campmeetings, leadership conferences, and church services around the world and across the United States.

Mark and Trina have written several books. For more information on Mark Hankins Ministries, log on to the website, www.markhankins.org.

PUBLICATIONS

✳ **SPIRIT-FILLED SCRIPTURE STUDY GUIDE**

A comprehensive study of scriptures in over 120 different translations on topics such as: Redemption, Faith, Finances, Prayer and more.

✳ **THE BLOODLINE OF A CHAMPION - THE POWER OF THE BLOOD OF JESUS**

The blood of Jesus is the liquid language of love that flows from the heart of God and gives us hope in all circumstances. In this book, you will clearly see what the blood has done FOR

US but also what the blood has done IN US as believers.

✳ TAKING YOUR PLACE IN CHRIST

Many Christians talk about what they are trying to be and what they are going to be. This book is about who <u>you are NOW as believers in Christ</u>.

✳ PAUL'S SYSTEM OF TRUTH

Paul's System of Truth reveals man's redemption in Christ, the reality of what happened from the cross to the throne and how it is applied for victory in life through Jesus Christ.

THE SECRET POWER OF JOY

If <u>you only knew what happens</u> <u>in the Spirit when you rejoice,</u> ! you would <u>rejoice everyday.</u> <u>Joy is</u> one of the <u>great secrets of</u> <u>faith.</u> This book will show you the importance of the joy of the Lord in a believer's life.

11:23 – THE LANGUAGE OF FAITH

Never underestimate the power of one voice. Over 100 inspirational, mountain-moving quotes to "stir up" the spirit of faith in you.

LET THE GOOD TIMES ROLL

This book focuses on the five key factors to heaven on earth: The

Holy Spirit, Glory, Faith, Joy, and Redemption. The Holy Spirit is a genius. If you will listen to Him, He will make you look smart.

THE POWER OF IDENTIFICATION WITH CHRIST

Learn how God identified us with Christ in His death, burial, resurrection, and seating in Heaven. The same identical life, victory, joy, and blessings that are In Christ are now in you. This is the glory and the mystery of Christianity – the power of the believer's identification with Christ.

REVOLUTIONARY REVELATION

This book provides excellent insight on how the spirit of wisdom and revelation is mandatory for believers to access their call, inheritance, and authority in Christ.

FAITH OPENS THE DOOR TO THE SUPERNATURAL

In this book you will learn how believing and speaking open the door to the supernatural.

THE SPIRIT OF FAITH

The Spirit of Faith is necessary to do the will of God and fulfill your divine destiny. Believing

AND speaking are necessary ingredients in the spirit of faith. If you ONLY knew what was on the other side of your mountain, you would move it!

DIVINE APPROVAL: UNDERSTANDING RIGHTEOUSNESS

The Gospel of Christ is a revelation of the righteousness of God, and the center of the Gospel reveals the righteousness of God. Understanding you have GOD'S DIVINE APPROVAL on your life sets you free from the sense of rejection, inadequacy or inferiority.

HOW TO RECEIVE GOD'S EXTRAVAGANT GENEROSITY

In this book, you will learn how to tap into God's supply and get results. When you are a generous giver, God does things for you that money cannot do— reaching beyond your finances into every area of your life.

NEVER RUN AT YOUR GIANT WITH YOUR MOUTH SHUT

The Bible story of David and Goliath gives us a picture of how faith in God is released through faith-filled words. Winning the War of words is necessary to win the fight of faith. Never underestimate the POWER of your voice!

GOD'S HEALING WORD
by Trina Hankins

Trina's testimony and a practical guide to <u>receiving healing</u> through meditating on the Word of God. This guide includes: testimonies, practical teaching, Scriptures & confessions, and a CD with Scriptures & confessions (read by Mark Hankins).

MARK HANKINS
MINISTRIES

P.O. Box 12863
Alexandria, LA 71315

318.767.2001

www.markhankins.org